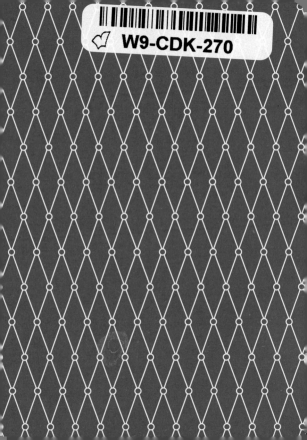

W9-CDK-270

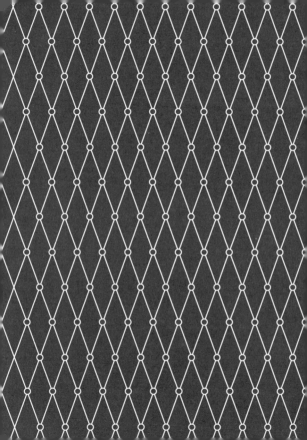

FORTUNE-TELLING BOOK
FOR MOMS-TO-BE

This book belongs to

_____

The gift of

_____

K. C. Jones

Illustrations by Fuko Kawamura

CHRONICLE BOOKS
SAN FRANCISCO

SECTION 1: PREGNANCY

"Life is always a rich and steady time when you are waiting for something to happen or to hatch."
—E. B. White

Life takes on a magical quality when you are awaiting the arrival of a baby; this wait is rich with portent, mystery, and promise. During the nine months of your pregnancy, you will have many opportunities to look forward to meeting your baby. Will it be a boy or a girl? What will he or she look like? Be like? You will have your own intuition about the baby you are carrying, and mothers' instincts are strong. But you should also look to the wisdom and tradition contained herein to learn more.

CONCEPTION

If you are trying to conceive and want to influence the sex of your baby, rely on these time-honored rituals. And if you are pregnant already, look to the following beliefs to see if you can divine any information about your child based on your activities around the time of conception. It is good luck to conceive a baby of either sex during a storm of any kind.

IF YOU WANT TO GIVE BIRTH TO A BOY

Seven days before conception eat carrots, mushrooms, tofu, and lettuce, and drink fizzy beverages.

Be sure always to eat breakfast around the time of conception, especially cereal.

Try to conceive on odd-numbered days of the month.

Sleep to the left of your partner.

Point your head north while trying to conceive.

Make love at night, especially when there is a quarter moon in the sky.

Place a knife under your bed.

Try this conception spell: Arrange three candles (one yellow, one green, and one blue) in a triangle, with the yellow candle at the top, the green to the left, and the blue to the right. Find an acorn and a dried leaf from an oak tree and place them in the center of the triangle of candles. Then repeat this incantation three times: "From this seed is born the sacred oak. From this union is born my beloved son." Place the acorn under your bed while trying to conceive.

IF YOU WANT TO GIVE BIRTH TO A GIRL

Seven days before conception eat fish, meat, nuts, and pickles and drink milk.

Try to conceive on even-numbered days of the month.

Sleep to the right of your partner.

Point your head south while trying to conceive.

Make love during the day, especially in the early afternoon, or at night under a full moon.

Place a wooden spoon, a skillet, or a pair of scissors under your bed.

Have your husband drink from a cracked glass: Legend has it that men who drink from cracked vessels will produce only girls.

Try this conception spell: Arrange three candles (one silver, one brown, and one blue) in a triangle, with the silver candle at the top of the triangle, the brown to the left, and the blue to the right. Find a rose with a thorny stem. Cut away the stem and place the rose in the center of the triangle of candles. Prick your index finger with a thorn from the stem and squeeze three drops of blood onto the rose.

Then repeat this incantation three times: "Sweet as the rose may be, and as strong as the thorn, from this union of flesh and spirit my daughter is born." Place the rose under your bed while trying to conceive.

AM I PREGNANT?

Other than the obvious symptoms—nausea, fatigue, food cravings—there are a few lesser-known signs that may indicate you are pregnant or will soon become pregnant.

A friend tells you she has dreamed of fish, or you yourself have a dream in which a fish appears.

You hold your arms in the air for several minutes and your fingertips remain warm but your hands and arms get cold.

Toddlers suddenly become drawn to you.

You are in the presence of a baby, and it starts to suck on its toes.

You find a pacifier on the ground or in a place where a baby does not live.

A baby looks at you from between its legs.

According to the 1639 book *An Alphabetical Book of Physical Secrets*, if a woman sees her reflection in her boiled urine, she is pregnant.

EATING FOR TWO

Maintaining a wholesome diet while you are pregnant not only helps you build a strong and healthy baby—it also can foretell characteristics of your child.

APPLES

For a rosy-cheeked baby, eat apples.

AVOCADO

For a healthy and beautiful child, eat avocado during your pregnancy.

BREAD

Do you prefer to eat from the middle of a loaf of bread? If so, you are most likely having a girl. A desire to eat the ends of the bread or the crust points to a boy.

CARROTS

Eating carrots will increase your chances of having a baby born with hair. Eating carrots cut into sticks also augurs good health for both you and your baby.

CILANTRO

Partaking of cilantro or coriander will lead to a pleasingly plump baby.

COCONUTS

Eating coconut meat or drinking coconut water will give your child a beautiful face and smooth skin.

COFFEE

Drinking coffee may mean you will give birth to a baby with birthmarks.

CRAB

Eating too much crab or shellfish during pregnancy will result in a mischievous child.

DATES

Dates boost fertility—even though you are already pregnant, you can increase your chances of having more children in the future by eating them.

EGGS

For a sharp-eyed baby, eat eggs. Eggs bring good fortune for a speedy and easy delivery—just be sure they are fully cooked.

FISH

For a graceful child, eat fish.

GARLIC

If you eat a raw clove of garlic and, hours later, a garlic smell seeps from your pores, get ready for a boy. If you do not smell garlic, you may be having a girl.

LEMONS

For a sweet baby, eat lemons.

MUSTARD

Avoid mustard—it can lead to a greedy child.

NUTMEG

Nutmeg will give you strength for your pregnancy and labor; in eighteenth-century England, pregnant women drank concoctions of nutmeg, eggs, sugar, and cinnamon.

PARSLEY

For a smart baby, eat parsley.

PASTA

Eating pasta (especially long, thin noodles) during pregnancy spells a long life for your baby.

PEACHES

Avoid peaches—they can make your infant overly hairy.

PEPPERS

If you eat spicy peppers during pregnancy, your baby may have a full head of hair at birth. The same is said for a mother-to-be who has heartburn.

ROSEMARY

Add rosemary to dishes while pregnant if you want to have many children. Rosemary will also increase the bonds of fidelity between you and your mate.

SAFFRON

For a pretty baby, eat saffron.

SNAILS

Avoid eating snails—they may make your child slow to walk.

STRAWBERRIES

Eating strawberries while pregnant will ensure that you and your baby will always have a close bond.

TEA

Taking your tea black increases your chances of having a redheaded child.

GENERAL CRAVINGS

Unfulfilled cravings during pregnancy may result in light brown birthmarks on the newborn's body. And any person who denies the craving of a pregnant woman will get a sty on his or her eye.

Cravings for savory, salty, or spicy foods signify a boy. Cravings for sweet foods or citrus fruits portend a girl.

Whatever you eat, cook it with care: Eating food that has been haphazardly prepared means the baby will have a careless nature. Also, try to avoid eating food directly from the pan or pot in which it was prepared; if you do, your baby may develop a stutter as he or she grows.

PREGNANCY SUPERSTITIONS

Pregnancy superstitions abound, from positive omens to rituals to ward off evil. While some of these may be nothing more than old wives' tales, it can't hurt to heed them if you're looking to increase your pregnancy luck.

Pregnancies run in the family: If your mother had easy pregnancies, you will most likely have an easy time as well. You will have stretch marks if she did, and if you were a large baby, you may give birth to a large baby as well!

If a pregnant woman steps over a hammock, her child will be born lazy.

If a pregnant woman stands idly in front of a full cupboard, her child will be greedy.

If a pregnant woman ties a cord around her waist, her child will be unlucky.

If you handle flowers too much, your child will have a weak sense of smell.

Always eat at a table; if you stand while eating, your baby will be gluttonous.

Never rock an empty cradle; this will lead to a baby who has difficulty sleeping.

A pregnant mother who often wears high heels may give birth to a cross-eyed child.

Avoid rubbing your pregnant belly too much; it is thought to lead to a child who is spoiled. (Having others touch or rub your belly has no effect, although it may be irksome to you!)

Europeans believe that everything planted in a garden by an expectant mother will grow well. So perhaps now is the time to get outside and sow some seeds.

FATHER-TO-BE

Though much of pregnancy lore focuses on the mother-to-be, there are a few signs that the father-to-be can watch out for and rituals he can undertake for good fortune.

If your mate goes out after dark while you are pregnant, he should not return directly home but instead go near the doorstep of a neighboring house first. This will throw any evil spirits who wish the baby harm off the scent.

It is unlucky for the father-to-be to cut his hair after his pregnant wife has passed her seventh month of pregnancy.

BOY OR GIRL?

What are you having? Though advances in science have made it possible to tell the sex of your baby around the fourth or fifth month, other methods have been used with success for thousands of years. Do not neglect them.

AGE AND YEAR

Compare your age at conception and the year that you conceived. If both are even numbers or odd numbers, the baby will be a girl. If one number is even, and one odd, it will be a boy. 29, 2012

Add together your age at conception and the year of conception. If the result is an even number, you are having a girl. If it is an odd number, a boy is coming.

29 + 2012 = 2041

BABY'S KICKS

If you first feel the baby kick on your left-hand side, it is a girl; if baby kicks on your right-hand side, it is a boy.

BEAUTY

Some cultures believe a baby girl "steals" the mother's beauty during the pregnancy. If you do not feel beautiful when you are pregnant, you may be having a girl. (Do not worry—after the birth you will be back to your previous lovely self.)

CHILD'S FIRST WORD

If you have a child already and his or her first word was "mama," your next baby will be a girl. If the child's first word was "dada," a boy is on the way.

COIN TEST

If you drop a coin between your breasts and it falls or rolls to your left, you will have a girl.

DREAMS

If you dream that you are having a boy, it is possible the end result will be a girl—and vice versa.

If you dream you are growing a beard, a girl is on the way. If you dream of eating sugar, you will give birth to a boy.

If you dream of a fountain or other running water, you will have a girl. If you dream of a knife or a hatchet, expect a boy. guns ?

If you see skulls or heads in your dream, your baby will be a boy; dreaming of flowers or feathers points to a girl.

DROPSY

If you are holding a knife and drop it, it is likely you will have a boy. If it is scissors you drop, a girl is on the way.

EGG TEST

Crack a raw egg onto your belly. To which direction does the egg slide off? If it slides to your right, you will be having a boy.

HEART RATE

If the baby's heart rate is above 140 beats per minute, it is said that the baby will be a girl. If it is under 140 beats per minute, then it will be a boy.

HOLIDAY VISITORS

If you are pregnant over the Christmas holiday, keep an eye out for the first person to enter your home on Christmas Eve—the sex of that person will be the sex of your baby.

HONEY WATER

Just before bed, drink a glass of water with a teaspoon of honey mixed in. If, when you wake up in the morning, you feel full on the left side of your stomach, you are carrying a girl.

INTEREST FROM BOYS

If a teenage male touches your belly without being prompted, it is likely you are having a boy. If a toddler boy expresses a great deal of interest in you, a girl is coming.

KEY TEST

Place a key on a table. Then close your eyes and reach for the key. If you pick it up at the top (the largest part), you will give birth to a boy. If you pick it up near the small end, a girl is on the way. If you pick it up right in the middle, twins are in your future!

MOOD SWINGS

Experiencing a range of emotions throughout the day on a regular basis can indicate a girl. A more even disposition means you are having a boy.

OWLS

If you hear an owl's hoot during your pregnancy, the baby will be a girl.

RING TEST

Tie your wedding ring to a strand of your hair or your partner's hair and hold the ring over your belly. If it swings in a circle, your child will be a boy. If it swings back and forth in a straight line, expect a girl. This test can also be performed with a threaded needle or a necklace.

ROOSTER

If you are in the presence of a rooster, and he crows while facing your dwelling, you are having a daughter. If the rooster crows facing away from the dwelling, the baby will be a boy.

SALIVA

If you notice your saliva is sweeter and thicker during pregnancy, you should expect a boy; saliva that tastes more bitter and watery than usual points to a girl.

SALT TEST

Place a grain or two of salt on your breast overnight. If, when you awake, the salt is dry, you will be having a boy. If it has liquefied, the baby is a girl!

SLEEPING POSITION

If you prefer to sleep on your left side during pregnancy, the baby may be a boy. *left side*

SNEEZING

If you are with another pregnant woman and you both sneeze in unison, you will give birth to daughters; if your husband sneezes in unison with another man, boys are on the way.

SPIDERWEBS

If you see a spiderweb, make a small hole in it with your finger. If the damage is repaired within the hour, a son is on the way; if the spider does not fix the hole quickly, you are having a girl.

TRIPPING

If you find that you are tripping over your own feet, or feeling unusually clumsy, it is likely you are having a boy.

CHINESE GENDER CHART

Legend has it that this chart was found buried in a royal tomb in China more than 700 years ago; it was recently said to have more than 90 percent accuracy. To use it, you must first discern in which Chinese lunar month conception took place. (The Chinese year begins with Chinese New Year, usually in January or February. Each month follows from there in a cycle of approximately 30 days, and are numbered from 1 to 12 consecutively.)

To use the chart on the next page, first determine the date of Chinese New Year in the year you conceived. Find your age at conception in the left column and the lunar month of conception in the top row, and look to the intersection of the two to determine the sex of your baby!

LUNAR MONTH OF CONCEPTION

	1	2	3	4	5
20	GIRL	BOY	GIRL	BOY	BOY
21	BOY	GIRL	GIRL	GIRL	GIRL
22	GIRL	BOY	BOY	GIRL	BOY
23	BOY	BOY	BOY	GIRL	BOY
24	BOY	GIRL	GIRL	BOY	BOY
25	GIRL	BOY	GIRL	BOY	GIRL
26	BOY	BOY	BOY	BOY	BOY
27	GIRL	GIRL	BOY	BOY	GIRL
28	BOY	BOY	BOY	GIRL	GIRL
29	GIRL	BOY	GIRL	GIRL	BOY
30	BOY	BOY	GIRL	BOY	GIRL
31	BOY	BOY	BOY	BOY	GIRL
32	BOY	GIRL	GIRL	BOY	GIRL
33	GIRL	BOY	BOY	GIRL	GIRL
34	BOY	BOY	GIRL	GIRL	BOY
35	BOY	GIRL	BOY	GIRL	BOY
36	BOY	GIRL	BOY	BOY	BOY
37	GIRL	GIRL	BOY	GIRL	GIRL
38	BOY	BOY	GIRL	GIRL	BOY
39	GIRL	GIRL	BOY	GIRL	GIRL
40	BOY	BOY	BOY	GIRL	BOY
41	GIRL	GIRL	BOY	GIRL	BOY
42	BOY	GIRL	GIRL	BOY	BOY
43	GIRL	BOY	GIRL	GIRL	BOY
44	BOY	GIRL	GIRL	GIRL	BOY
45	GIRL	BOY	GIRL	BOY	GIRL

AGE AT CONCEPTION

6	7	8	9	10	11	12
BOY	GIRL	BOY	GIRL	BOY	BOY	BOY
GIRL	BOY	GIRL	GIRL	GIRL	GIRL	GIRL
GIRL	GIRL	BOY	BOY	GIRL	BOY	GIRL
BOY	BOY	BOY	BOY	GIRL	BOY	BOY
GIRL	BOY	GIRL	GIRL	BOY	BOY	GIRL
BOY	GIRL	BOY	GIRL	BOY	GIRL	BOY
GIRL	BOY	BOY	BOY	BOY	BOY	GIRL
BOY	GIRL	GIRL	BOY	BOY	GIRL	BOY
BOY	BOY	BOY	BOY	GIRL	GIRL	BOY
GIRL	GIRL	BOY	GIRL	GIRL	BOY	GIRL
BOY	BOY	BOY	GIRL	BOY	GIRL	BOY
GIRL	BOY	BOY	BOY	BOY	GIRL	GIRL
BOY	BOY	GIRL	GIRL	BOY	GIRL	BOY
BOY	GIRL	BOY	BOY	GIRL	GIRL	BOY
GIRL	BOY	BOY	GIRL	GIRL	BOY	GIRL
GIRL	BOY	GIRL	BOY	GIRL	BOY	GIRL
GIRL	BOY	GIRL	BOY	BOY	BOY	GIRL
GIRL	GIRL	GIRL	BOY	GIRL	GIRL	GIRL
GIRL	BOY	BOY	GIRL	GIRL	BOY	GIRL
GIRL	GIRL	GIRL	BOY	GIRL	GIRL	GIRL
GIRL	BOY	BOY	BOY	GIRL	BOY	GIRL
BOY	GIRL	GIRL	BOY	GIRL	BOY	BOY
BOY	BOY	GIRL	GIRL	BOY	BOY	BOY
BOY	GIRL	BOY	GIRL	GIRL	BOY	BOY
GIRL	BOY	GIRL	GIRL	GIRL	BOY	GIRL
GIRL	GIRL	BOY	GIRL	BOY	GIRL	GIRL

ACHES AND PAINS

Pregnancy comes with its fair share of physical symptoms. While they may be uncomfortable, look on the bright side: You can use many of the symptoms to predict the gender of your unborn child.

BREASTS

If your right breast is firmer than your left during pregnancy, the baby will be a boy—and vice versa.

If your left breast is larger than your right during pregnancy, the baby will be a girl—and vice versa. *left = bigger*

EYES

If your right eye shines more brightly than your left, the baby will be a boy.

Pull down the skin under your left eye. If the veins in the white part of your eye form a "V" shape, your baby will be a girl.

FACE

If you feel like your nose is growing or getting wider, it might mean you're carrying a boy.

If you are experiencing an increase in acne or pesky break-outs, this points to a girl. *yes*

If your face becomes fuller and rounder, the baby is most likely a girl; a long and narrow face means a boy.

FEET

If you notice that your feet are colder than usual, that points to a boy.

HAIR

If the hair on your body (especially your legs) has been growing faster than normal, you are most likely having a boy. *slower*

If the hair on your head develops red highlights, expect a girl.

HANDS

Dry, chapped hands during pregnancy portend a boy.

HEAD

Having more headaches than normal during pregnancy signifies a baby boy. *less then normal (9/12)*

STOMACH

Morning sickness often signifies the baby will be a girl. So if you have had a fairly smooth and nausea-free pregnancy, ready the nursery for a boy. *no sickness yet*

If you feel heaviness in the lower or front part of your stomach, signs point to a boy. If you feel pressure higher up or in the middle of your stomach, it is a girl.

GENDER TESTS FOR OTHERS
TO PERFORM

Mom-to-be, do not read the text that follows, for the answers depend on your honest, unbiased reactions. Give this book to your partner, a friend, or a family member, and let that person help you determine the sex of your baby.

Ask a pregnant woman to hold out her hands. If she holds them palm up, she is having a girl; palm down, it's a boy.

Call to a pregnant woman from behind. If she turns and looks at you over her left shoulder, the baby is a boy; the right shoulder, a girl.

An older woman should throw a pinch of salt into the pregnant woman's hair when she is unsuspecting. If she touches her forehead first, expect a boy; if she touches her chin first, a girl is on the way.

Place parsley on the mother-to-be's head without her knowledge. If it remains on her head and the first person she speaks to afterward is a male, the baby will be a boy—and vice versa. If the parsley falls off, the test is inconclusive.

Offer a pregnant woman both a rose and a lily. If she chooses the rose, it points to a girl child; the lily means a boy.

AM I HAVING TWINS?

If you went swimming on the first day you were married, twins are likely in your future. *yes!*

If you saw a movie or play in a theater within three days of your wedding, you should also prepare for twins. *no*

MOOD SWINGS

It is normal for your emotions to be all over the place during pregnancy. Here is what some of these mood swings mean.

If you argue with your mother or mother-in-law during pregnancy, your labor and delivery will be more difficult. Small disagreements will not affect you, but stay away from thorny issues until after the child is born.

Funerals and weddings are thought to cause strong mood swings in pregnant women that can affect the unborn baby, so if you must attend these events while you are pregnant, try to keep your emotions as in check as possible.

Do not hold grudges while pregnant, lest your baby come out resembling the person you hold the grudge against.

Using curse words while you are pregnant may make your baby cursed as well.

Being close to water will help ease your moods during pregnancy.

BABY DREAMS

Pregnant women often report having extremely vivid dreams. These dreams hold meaning. Read on to learn more.

PREDICTING YOUR DUE DATE

While your doctor will provide you with a due date, here are some other ways to know when baby will come. Conventional wisdom holds that your baby will be born within 150 days of the day you first feel him or her move inside you. So mark the date you first feel a stirring in your tummy, and count out 150 days from there. Then wait to see which due date is more accurate!

If you have a nightmare in which you are in danger or are being threatened, and in the dream you take control and get yourself out of the situation, you will have a short and easy labor.

Dreams of being enclosed in a small space may signify a fear of being robbed of freedom by your baby.

If you dream of eating large amounts of food, it means your child will be a good eater.

Dreaming of your unborn child means that the two of you will have a strong bond after the birth.

If you dream of missing an appointment, you may subconsciously feel that you are not up to the challenge of motherhood. However, you need not worry.

If a newborn appears in your dream, and he or she is talking or otherwise doing things beyond its age, it is a sign that your own child will go far.

NESTING INSTINCT

During pregnancy, especially in its later stages, many women feel an urge to prepare the house for baby. Read on to learn how to use this work to your advantage—and which nesting instincts should be avoided.

BABY GEAR

The Chinese believe it is bad luck to have an empty stroller in the house before the baby is born. So if you buy one, store it at the home of a friend or relative until the birth.

The same goes for new baby clothes—it is better luck to store them elsewhere until after the infant is born. Baby clothes that have been used before carry with them good luck and protective powers. Ask your friends and family for hand-me-downs.

Knitting during pregnancy can cause confusion for the unborn child. If you are knitting baby items, do so out of the house. Better yet, see if friends or family will take on knitting projects for you.

FENG SHUI

Ensure that any frayed electrical wires are replaced and improperly functioning outlets fixed—a smooth flow of electricity throughout a dwelling promotes a smooth pregnancy.

Work to keep your home clean and uncluttered, especially around your bed. An untidy home can contribute to an unstable pregnancy.

The bedroom should be brightly lit, preferably by sunlight, when you are not sleeping.

The presence of water in the home adds a relaxing element to a pregnancy. Consider adding a fountain or a fish tank.

Use colors to promote a healthy pregnancy—positive hues are light blue, dark blue, green, and red. Paint rooms in these colors, or add furniture in these tones to your home.

Use essential oils around the home to foster an easy pregnancy: Chamomile, rosemary, jasmine, marjoram, bergamot, and fennel all do the trick. Or cook with these herbs and spices for a similar benefit.

Precious stones like citrine, quartz, tourmaline, and carnelian promote positive energy and good health in a home during a pregnancy—place these stones throughout your rooms.

Images of babies hung around the house will protect your unborn child.

HOME RENOVATIONS AND PROJECTS

If you begin a project around the house while pregnant, it is important that you not leave it unfinished; to do so would prolong your labor.

Chinese superstition holds that the spirit of an unborn child roams the house where it is to live, and that, if the mom-to-be uses tools to work on the house, it could be harmful to that spirit. If any renovation work needs to be done, hand the hammer, pliers, drill, or saw to the father-to-be.

Using glue during pregnancy may bring on a difficult labor. While you are pregnant, use tape, staples, or paper clips instead.

Similarly, tying knots while pregnant is not recommended, as it may make labor more difficult.

HOUSEKEEPING

If a pregnant woman uses her apron to dust anything, she will have a boisterous child.

Legend has it that if a pregnant woman dips her hands in dirty water, her children will be born with coarse hands—more incentive for you to have your partner do the dishes during pregnancy!

It is bad luck for a mother-to-be to extinguish a fire in the fireplace—have another family member take on this task.

IN THE BEDROOM

It is bad luck to move your bed during pregnancy; wait until after the baby is born.

Using scissors while sitting in bed is a bad omen during pregnancy. If you clip coupons or articles, do it at the table instead.

While you are pregnant, avoid sleeping in total darkness, as it can leave you and your baby susceptible to dark spirits. A small night-light should do the trick.

If you and your partner are having marital difficulties during your pregnancy, place a pearl under your pillow while you sleep, and tensions will ease.

MOVING HOUSE

While you are pregnant, do not visit houses that have been vacant for a long while; they may contain dangerous spirits that can affect you or your baby. If you are considering moving, have your partner or other family members take pictures of prospective houses for you, or make sure houses are full of furniture when you visit.

ANIMAL OMENS

Members of the animal kingdom hold special portent when it comes to pregnancy.

Seeing a bird's nest or wasp's nest attached to your dwelling is very good luck and bodes well for an easy and quick labor and delivery.

If a pregnant woman hears an owl hoot outside her house at night and she is the only one who hears the call, her baby will be blessed throughout life.

Seeing a donkey during pregnancy is a good omen for a future well-behaved child.

Scorpion bites during pregnancy are actually lucky, as they are thought to immunize baby against bites in the future.

Stepping over a black cat during pregnancy is very lucky, but only if it happens accidentally—you cannot go seeking out black cats to step over! Stepping over any other color cat does not hold the same luck.

If a rat runs around your feet while you are pregnant, it is a bad omen. Mice are good luck, however!

If a ferret or weasel jumps over the stomach of a pregnant woman—an unlikely event unless you happen to have one of these animals as a pet—then her child may be born with a birthmark.

Stay away from zoos while you are pregnant—some people believe that wild animals can become enraged and uncontrollable in the presence of a pregnant woman.

PREGNANCY RITUALS
AROUND THE WORLD

Pregnancy rituals abound in the different cultures of the world. Read on to learn more; you might even decide to try out one or two.

Canadian Eskimos believe that the baby has a spirit from early on in the pregnancy; the mother-to-be is encouraged to talk to the baby, because it can learn from her even before it is born.

In a Malay mother-to-be's seventh month, her friends and family create a doll out of flowers to resemble a baby. The doll is sprinkled with rice paste, placed in a cradle, sung to, and then passed around to all the relatives to be held. The doll stays in the cradle overnight, after which it is broken up and thrown into water. This ritual is meant to ease labor and delivery for the mother.

The Chagga people of Tanzania revere pregnant women. A traditional Chagga saying is, "Pay attention to the pregnant woman, for there is no one more important than she."

During an Indian woman's pregnancy, a traditional ceremony is held, attended by female friends and relatives. The mother-to-be wears a new silk sari and all her best jewelry, and her feet and hands are decorated with henna. She sits in a large, comfortable chair, and all the attendees who have given birth go up to her and adorn her arms with bangles, blessing her so she will deliver a healthy baby. After the celebration, the mother-to-be proceeds to her mother's house, where she stays until she gives birth.

In many African cultures, families perform rituals to protect pregnancies, believing that evil spirits can gain access to the unborn baby and hurt him or her. Because of this, pregnancy is not generally celebrated or talked about in public, lest the spirits become aware of it. For the same reason, African mothers-to-be often do not accept gifts before their babies are born.

A SPELL FOR A HEALTHY BABY

Cut an apple in half and rub one cut half over your bare belly. While doing so, visualize any pain and sickness being drawn from your belly into the apple. Bury the apple half in the ground outside your home. Once back inside, light a green candle, and slice and eat the other apple half, envisioning your happy, healthy child. Performing this ritual will keep your child safe.

If the buried apple grows into a tree, this is an especially good omen and means your child will never go hungry.

KEEPING EVIL AWAY

Many traditions and cultures believe that as an unborn baby grows, it is very close to the spirit world, making both mother and baby susceptible to evil spirits. Try these rituals to keep yourself and baby safe.

Wearing perfume when you go out at night will keep bad spirits away.

Keeping an object made of metal—such as a nail, a pair of scissors, or a necklace—on your person will ward off evil.

To keep baby safe during pregnancy, bathe each Friday in water to which the juice of limes has been added.

To protect your unborn baby from evil spirits, place a knife under your bed. (If you were trying to conceive a boy, you may already have a knife under your bed!)

Cross your fingers when you are around people you distrust or who wish you evil; this will ward off their bad spirits.

Shoelaces act as protective amulets during pregnancy, so wear shoes that tie rather than shoes that slip on.

Rose oil or rosewater offers protection to pregnant women; sprinkle it over household items to keep baby safe.

A child's tooth is a good luck charm—wear it on a necklace or in a pouch around your neck, and you will bear strong and healthy children.

Place a few caraway seeds in a pouch or sachet and carry them with you wherever you go to ward off spirits who may wish evil upon you or your baby.

Mix cumin and salt together and scatter around the perimeter of your house to protect all who dwell within.

PRECIOUS STONES

Amulets and charms made from certain stones bear good luck:

- ❖ Toadstones protect pregnant women from demons.

- ❖ Rose quartz protects and calms during pregnancy.

- ❖ Blue stones, like sapphire and aquamarine, guard against evil during pregnancy.

- ❖ Amber keeps mothers and unborn children safe from harm.

GODS AND GODDESSES OF PREGNANCY AND CHILDBIRTH

Summon these gods and goddesses from different cultures to watch over and help you during your pregnancy.

AFRICAN

Ala: Nigerian goddess of creation

Yemaya: goddess of the ocean and fertility

Erzulie Freda: Yoruban goddess of love, sex, and fertility

Oshun: goddess of rivers and fertility

Shango: god of twins

CENTRAL AMERICAN

Ixchel: Mayan goddess of medicine, fertility, and miracles

Chaac: Mayan fertility rain god

CHINESE

Ch'ang O: goddess of the moon and fertility

Kwan Yin: goddess of mercy

EGYPTIAN

Taweret: a midwife goddess who aids in childbirth

Isis: goddess of fertility and motherhood

Bes: a dwarf god who keeps newborns entertained and stops their crying

Hathor: fertility goddess and protector of pregnant women

EUROPEAN

Aine: Celtic goddess of love, wealth, and fertility

Freya: Nordic goddess of love and fertility

Brighid: Celtic/Irish goddess of the home, hearth, and fertility

St. Catherine: Swedish patron saint who prevents miscarriages

St. Gerard Majella: patron saint of pregnancy and mothers-to-be

St. Raymund Nonnatus: patron saint of midwives

GREEK

Artemis: moon goddess and goddess who protects all animals, including humans, during childbirth

Demeter: the goddess of single mothers

Hera: mother of all the gods, she protects women and mothers

INDIAN

Ganesha: remover of obstacles in childbirth

Sarasvati: goddess of rivers and fertility

Shiva: god of medicine and fertility

JAPANESE

Kannon: goddess of mercy, love, and fertility

ROMAN

Opigena: aids in childbirth

Natio: aids in childbirth

Vaticanus: helps stop the crying of newborns

Educa: provides food for the baby

Rumina: goddess of breast-feeding

Cunina: guardian of the cradle

Statulinus: helps newborns to walk

Lucina: aids mothers in labor

Partula: presides over delivery

Carmenta: predicts the future of newborns

Levana: protects the child; ensures that the father accepts the child

Locutius: teaches babies to speak

RULING PLANETS IN PREGNANCY

While you are pregnant, celestial bodies are watching over you. Learn what to expect in each month of your pregnancy.

WEEKS 1-4

Venus: Venus represents love, beauty, and fertility, and watches over the beginning of a pregnancy.

WEEKS 5-8

Mars: Mars is the god of war and keeps pregnant women safe during the second month of pregnancy. Tuesday is Mars's day, so during your second month, try and schedule any appointments or doctor's visits on that day.

WEEKS 9-12

Jupiter: Jupiter brings luck, happiness, and optimism to the third month of pregnancy—just what you may need as you are finishing up your first trimester.

WEEKS 13-16

The Sun: As you head into your second trimester, the sun warms and protects your growing baby. And as its name suggests, Sunday is the sun's day, so keep your eye out for positive pregnancy omens on Sundays during your fourth month.

WEEKS 17-20

The Moon: The moon, especially a full moon, rules this month. And Monday, "the moon's day," is the most auspicious day of this fifth month. Look for good things to happen on Mondays.

WEEKS 21-24

Saturn: Saturn represents abundance, peace, serenity, and wisdom—expect these characteristics to enter your life in your sixth month of pregnancy, especially on Saturdays ("Saturn's day").

WEEKS 25-28

Mercury: Mercury is associated with flights of fancy and quick changes in mood. In your seventh month, expect to feel a bit scattered and moody. But do not fear, for the eighth month will bring more calm.

WEEKS 29–36

The Sun: The sun reenters the scene for your eighth and ninth months, bringing warmth to your body and helping your baby grow to his or her full potential before birth. Again, look to Sundays for auspicious events.

WEEKS 37–40

The Moon: Just as the moon affects ocean tides, it is believed that the moon's gravitational pull has a particular effect on pregnant women, especially on the amniotic fluid just before delivery. Many babies are born under a full moon.

SECTION 2: THE BIRTH

"Birth is the sudden opening of a window, through which you look out upon a stupendous prospect. For what has happened? A miracle. You have exchanged nothing for the possibility of everything."
—William MacNeile Dixon

It is true; childbirth is nothing short of a miracle. And women's wisdom from years gone by has much to teach us. In this section, you will find age-old tips and tricks to ease and quicken labor, time-tested labor and delivery rituals, and how details about the birth process and your new baby can speak volumes about his or her future.

LABOR AND DELIVERY

Part of a natural childbirth means going through labor. Read on to discover ways to speed and ease this process, and how aspects of the birth hold clues to your baby's fate.

FOR AN EASY DELIVERY

Before you go into labor, have your partner carry you over a pan of burning coals near the threshold to your home. Doing this ensures trouble-free labor.

Tradition holds that everything that is locked or tied up or otherwise bound should be undone during a woman's labor; this represents the baby's easy trip through the birth canal, with no blockages.

So, before you give birth, do the following:

❖ Open all windows.

❖ Open doors. (Doors to the outside may remain closed for safety as long as windows are open.)

❖ Unlock all locks.

❖ Uncork all bottles.

❖ Untie any knots or shoelaces, especially on your own clothing or shoes.

❖ Unbutton all buttons, especially on baby clothes.

❖ Loosen ties and belts.

Along the same lines, all women in a house or hospital room where a baby is being born should loosen their hair or take it out of buns, braids, and ponytails. Keep this in mind if you have female relatives with you during the delivery.

After you have given birth, everything should be tied, locked, knotted, and tightened again as soon as possible, or else the newborn's soul can be stolen by fairies. Tradition holds that windows and doors should be kept closed for the first forty days of a child's life.

TO BRING ON LABOR

If you are nearing your due date and have not gone into labor, some believe that going on a bumpy car ride (not too bumpy, of course, and wear your seat belt!) can bring on the first contractions.

If a full moon is coming soon and you are near your due date, you may be in luck; the full moon has the ability to call forth babies.

Walk up and down several flights of stairs to start labor.

Have a horse eat out of your apron—this will bring on labor and make it easy to boot. If you do not have a horse nearby, a domestic pet makes an acceptable substitute.

Strew rose petals on the floor, making a path from your bedroom to your unborn baby's room, and walk back and forth between the rooms, on the petals, several times a day.

Ask a red-haired friend for a few strands of her hair. Place them in a small bag and carry it with you, next to your belly, toward the end of your pregnancy. It will bring you good luck and a speedy labor.

FOODS AND DRINKS
TO SUMMON LABOR

Peppermint tea

Tea made from raspberry leaf

Tea with black pepper in it

Warm water with a dash of peanut oil in it

Balsamic vinegar

Anything containing cumin

Spicy curry

TO SPEED YOUR LABOR
ONCE IT HAS BEGUN

To quicken your labor, drink from a cup from which another woman has recently drunk. If the other woman is a mother, all the better, and if she has recently given birth, that is the best situation of all.

When you are in labor, do not sit at the top or bottom of a set of stairs, and ask family members to do the same. Sitting on stairs will prolong labor and delivery. The same goes for standing in doorways.

Some tribes in Japan believe that a mother who has exercised during pregnancy will have a shorter labor as her reward. So if you are reading this while still pregnant, take heed!

If the labor is progressing slowly, have the father-to-be place paper money under your pillow, and see if this does not move things along. After the delivery, the money should be given to charity as a show of gratitude.

TO EASE LABOR PAIN

Shortly before your due date, make a practice of throwing salt behind you once a day. This will ease your future labor. And while you are laboring, hold a small amount of salt clenched in each of your fists; it will give you strength.

Used together, aventurine, chrysoprase, amethyst, and quartz have pain-easing powers. Keep one each of these four stones in the room where you will be delivering, or wear them in a small pouch around your neck. After the baby is born, increase your luck by giving the stones away as gifts—they will do the most good if given to someone who is pregnant or trying to become pregnant.

Leave an ax or other blade by your bed or in the room where you will give birth; it is thought to "cut the pain."

If you are in pain during labor, lie down and have the father-to-be or a male relative walk over your stomach three times, back and forth.

The smell of cedar, mugwort, or amber is said to relieve labor pains.

Put on your mate's slippers if your labor is painful; this is thought to transfer strength from the man to the woman and pain from the woman to the man. (And surely he will not mind sharing some of your pain!)

Place two twigs in a cross or X-shape (hazel twigs are best), and place them under your pillow to ease labor pain.

LABOR AROUND THE WORLD

In late-nineteenth-century Europe, church bells were rung to hasten labor and delivery.

If their labor was moving slowly, Klamath tribeswomen spoke to their unborn babies, telling them that snakes were coming to bite them if they did not hurry to be born.

Among the Dayak people of Borneo, a medicine man and his assistant visit women who are having difficult labor. The assistant stands outside the woman's home with a white stone, and the medicine man directs him to move the stone in the air, using the same movements the medicine man is using as he massages the woman's belly.

Yucatecan women in Mexico are often given a raw egg to swallow if their labor is progressing slowly.

In nineteenth-century Russia, pregnant women and their husbands were made to name the people with whom they had slept. If the woman's labor was easy, it was assumed that both had told the truth. If it was difficult, it was believed one of them had not been truthful.

Traditionally, Arabic women practiced belly dancing while pregnant as a way to ready their bodies for labor. During labor, tribeswomen would dance with a pregnant woman to hypnotize her, help her forget the pain, and help her move with her contractions.

In colonial America, a woman in labor would often sit on her husband's lap, and he would hold her under the arms or around the stomach. Though this could become tiresome for the husband, it was believed to be the least he could do, because he was in part responsible for the coming baby!

In Bangladesh, women place an old knife, an old shoe, and a broomstick under the bed where a baby is being born to ward off evil spirits.

LABOR SUPERSTITIONS

Turtles should be kept away from the room where a mother is in labor, as they are thought to impede delivery.

A string or thread tied around a laboring mother's wrist will prevent her soul from escaping during the delivery.

It is bad luck for a dog or cat to cross the roof of a house where a baby is being born; to prevent this, keep your animals inside. In fact, having a cat in the house during a birth is a lucky omen.

Using a broom in the delivery room is believed to sweep away all the luck of the newborn baby. Save sweeping until one day after the birth.

A piece of iron placed in the birthing bed will protect mother and child during the delivery. The same holds true for a bowl or pan of water placed under the bed.

With each person the mother-to-be speaks to after labor begins, the laboring process is prolonged; therefore, you might want to limit the number of people you see during labor and delivery.

After a woman has gone into labor, no coal, ash, or embers may be removed from the fireplace in her home; this is bad luck for the baby.

It is also bad luck for a mom-to-be to lend out anything on the day she goes into labor. Just to be on the safe side, stop lending before your due date.

Rings and bracelets are thought to be protective amulets during labor and delivery. Taking them off during labor can leave the mother-to-be vulnerable to evil spirits and witches.

BIRTH AROUND THE WORLD

Aboriginal women in Australia give birth without any men present. When labor begins, female elders escort her away from her home, and she gives birth outside on the land. This is thought to create a special bond between the mother, child, and Earth.

Yucatecan women in Mexico give birth while sitting or lying in a hammock. Men, especially the father-to-be, are expected to be close by during the birth and are blamed if they are absent and the labor and delivery is difficult.

Native American new mothers traditionally submerged themselves and their babies in water just after birth. This was meant to serve as the baby's first initiation into the trials and tribulations of life.

In the nineteenth century, pregnant women on the Indonesian island of Ceram gave birth with their hands above their heads tied to a tree; they believed this made for a quick delivery.

After a birth in the Philippines, the baby's umbilical cord is often cut to a length that, when stretched, can touch the baby's forehead. This is believed to make the baby wise.

Similarly, Sumatrans often cut the umbilical cord with a flute, believing it leads to children who are musically inclined.

HOW BABY IS BORN

Breech babies have healing powers and often possess second sight, the ability to see into the future. They will bring luck to their family.

Caesarean section babies are beautiful as adults and will have fewer struggles in life. But they have a tendency toward laziness.

Babies who are born with their face turned downward will have the ability to see into the future.

Premature babies are independent, energetic, impatient, and ambitious as adults.

Babies born well after their due date will be good sleepers, although as they grow into adulthood, they may have a tendency toward selfishness and depression.

Babies born after long labors will be patient and methodical people, although they can be stubborn.

Babies born after quick labors will be easygoing in nature, if somewhat flighty and fickle.

THE PLACENTA

In many cultures, the placenta, or afterbirth, is considered an essential part of the baby's being, soul, and spirit; it is often buried near the family's dwelling for good outcomes:

❖ Bury the placenta near the back door of a house, and baby will always have enough food and possessions. Buried near the threshold of a home, the placenta will keep the family safe from fire and other disasters.

❖ Bury it under the hearth, and baby will have a strong love of home.

❖ Bury it under a fruit tree for a girl's future fertility, and a nut tree for a boy's.

❖ Bury the placenta at the foot of a young small tree, and the child will grow as the tree grows.

THE UMBILICAL CORD

The umbilical cord, the baby's link to its mother, is another prized possession in many cultures, and beliefs about how it should be handled after birth abound:

- ❖ Burning the umbilical cord will give baby independence, calm, and self-possession.

- ❖ If the umbilical cord is kept in a jar, the child will live a very long time.

- ❖ If the cord is wrapped in cloth and buried, baby will be safe from evil all her life.

- ❖ If the cord is buried close to home, baby will remain loyal to his parents always.

- ❖ If umbilical cords from successive children are kept in the same place, the siblings will always be close and will not argue.

- ❖ If the umbilical cord stump drops off in less than seven days, baby will always feel hungry. If it takes more than seven days, she will be able to go a long time without eating or feeling hunger.

WHEN BABY ARRIVES

The date, the day, and even the time of day a baby is born can all foretell information about his or her future.

BIRTH TIME OF DAY

If a baby is born at night, she will be a nocturnal creature and have a habit of staying up late.

If a child is born in the morning, the opposite will be true—he will be an early riser.

Babies born at three, six, nine, or twelve o'clock on the dot are said to be exceptionally lucky and will grow up to have ingenuity and insight in spades. They also have a mysterious power over animals.

A baby born in the last few minutes before the clock strikes midnight will have supernatural abilities and be able to see ghosts.

A child born in the first minutes after midnight will be blessed with eternal luck.

BIRTH DAY OF THE WEEK

Monday's child will always seek the truth and will be gentle and calm. He will be kind but occasionally possessive and somewhat overemotional.

Lucky color: White

Tuesday's child will be attractive to the opposite sex and courageous, independent, and strong. She will be hot-tempered and impatient.

Lucky color: Red

Wednesday's child will be intelligent and studious, perceptive and communicative, though somewhat careless and unreliable.

Lucky color: Purple

Thursday's child will be blessed with kindness and compassion. He will be practical, generous, and cheerful, though often hypocritical and obsessive. He will marry late in life.

Lucky color: Blue

Friday's child will be lighthearted and articulate, have a real talent for music, and a taste for luxurious items. She may be less than scrupulous in business matters. This child will also have a tendency to marry late in life.

Lucky color: Green

Saturday's child will have a professional bearing and much wisdom and dedication to any task undertaken. In his personal life, though, he will be rather timid and quiet, and somewhat prone to complaining.

Lucky color: Black

Sunday's child will be outgoing and brave, and an intrepid traveler. She will be successful in business, although a tad egotistical and overbearing. Evil spirits will never touch this child.

Lucky color: Yellow

Children born between Friday midnight and dawn on Saturday will have magical powers.

Old English nursery rhymes that augur a child's future based on the day of the week of his or her birth abound. Here are a few of them.

Born on Monday, fair in the face;
Born on Tuesday, full of God's grace;
Born on Wednesday, the best to be had;
Born on Thursday, merry and glad;
Born on Friday, worthily given;
Born on Saturday, work hard for a living;
Born on Sunday, shall never know want.

Monday's child is fair of face;
Tuesday's child is full of grace;
Wednesday's child is full of woe;
Thursday's child has far to go;
Friday's child is loving and giving;
Saturday's child works hard for a living.
But the child that is born on the Sabbath day
is fair and wise, good and gay.

Sunday's child is full of grace;
Monday's child is fair of face;
Tuesday's child loves to race;
Wednesday's child is kind of heart;
Thursday's child is very smart;
Friday's child will never part;
Saturday's child is good of heart.

SPECIAL BIRTH DATES

Babies born on January 1 are said to be the luckiest of all throughout their lives and possess the double gifts of foresight and hindsight.

January 14 babies can communicate with the supernatural.

January children will protect their whole household against the evil eye.

February 29 babies have exceptional luck (even though their birthday falls only once every four years).

Children born on Easter Sunday will be wealthy and joyful.

March 22 babies will always be thirsty.

Babies born on April 1 will have luck in life, as long as they avoid gambling.

April newborns will be stubborn and a bit unpredictable.

June babies will be very energetic and lively adults.

July 19 children will be strong.

September 27 boy infants will be fond of women and drink as they grow older.

Babies born on October 31 can communicate with the spirit world and are protected against evil.

December 25 children will be talented and generous.

MOON CYCLES

When a child is born under a waning moon, the next birth will be a child of the opposite sex. When a child is born under a waxing moon, the next birth will be a child of the same sex.

BIRTH ORDER

To be the seventh child is extraordinarily lucky.

A first, third, or fifth girl is lucky.

A fifth- or sixth-born girl will bring prosperity to her family.

If the baby is your first, he or she will be interested in intellectual pursuits (the same goes for only children). Firstborns are dutiful and responsible.

Second-born or third-born children have a predilection toward artistic careers. They enjoy the outdoors and nature.

Fourth-born or fifth-born children have a drive to excel.

IT'S TWINS!

If you are doubly blessed, be thankful, for twins possess special characteristics—some even say they have mystical and magical powers.

Twins have power to control weather.

Twins can be immune to snakebites and scorpion stings.

Many twins have healing powers and can cure diseases.

Generally, the first twin will be more ambitious and dominant; the second twin will be more content to sit back and let others take the lead.

It is believed that if twins are spoiled, the whole family will prosper.

NUMEROLOGY

Numbers, including the date of a baby's birth, can influence the future course of his or her life and provide insight into the child and adult he or she will become. Using numerology, it is possible to divine these insights.

Use the date of your baby's birth as a starting point to determine a final number that will govern his or her life. To begin, you will need to add the numbers of the birth date together. For example, if the birth date is October 18, 2011 (10/18/2011), break the numbers into single digits so that you are adding them as follows:

$1 + 0 + 1 + 8 + 2 + 0 + 1 + 1 = 14.$

Since 14 is a two-digit number, you'll need to break it down further to arrive at the final number. So add the numerals in 14 together:

$1 + 4 = 5.$

5 is the final number.

Note if the sum of the birth date digits is 11 or 22, you do not need to break these numbers down further.

Here is what the numbers mean:

1 = Creative, independent, original, adventurous,
    yet egotistical

2 = Empathetic, diplomatic, sensitive, intuitive, cautious,
    yet codependent

3 = Artistic, enthusiastic, visionary, optimistic, sociable,
    yet superficial and wasteful

4 = Organized, efficient, practical, loyal, serious, yet rigid

5 = Creative, inventive, free-spirited, adaptable,
    yet volatile

6 = Responsible, understanding, loving, passionate,
    harmonious, yet jealous

7 = Intuitive, spiritual, wise, analytical, yet critical
    and isolated

8 = Powerful, decisive, authoritative, organized,
    yet materialistic

9 = Compassionate, generous, romantic, imaginative,
    devoted, yet overemotional

11 and 22 are "master numbers" and their characteristics are as follows:

11 = Creative, idealistic, inventive, wise, yet insensitive.
An 11 can also have characteristics of a 2, since 1 + 1 = 2.

22 = Innovative, driven, practical, masterful, yet harsh.
A 22 can also have characteristics of a 4, since 2 + 2 = 4.

ASTROLOGY

Your baby's birthday also determines his or her astrological sign, which can predict personality characteristics, lucky items, and the other signs he or she will be compatible with later in life.

IF YOUR BIRTHDAY FALLS ON OR BETWEEN THESE DATES . . . *	YOUR ASTROLOGICAL SIGN IS . . .
March 22–April 21	Aries
April 22–May 21	Taurus
May 22–June 21	Gemini
June 22–July 21	Cancer
July 22–August 21	Leo
August 22–September 21	Virgo
September 22–October 21	Libra
October 22–November 21	Scorpio
November 22–December 21	Sagittarius
December 22–January 21	Capricorn
January 22–February 21	Aquarius
February 22–March 21	Pisces

*If the birthday is two to three days from the beginning or end of a date range, baby is said to be "on the cusp," meaning that he or she may also display characteristics of the sign that precedes or follows the sign, as well as the characteristics of his or her own sign.

ARIES

❖ Birthday: March 22–April 21 ❖

Aries Key Traits: Independent, optimistic, courageous, generous, impatient, short-tempered, impulsive

Element: Fire

Animal: Ram

Body Parts Governed: Head and face

Ruling Planet: Mars

Lucky Numbers: 1, 2, 4, 9

Lucky Colors: Deep red, green

Lucky Gemstones: Amethyst, diamond, ruby

Lucky Flowers: Dahlia, peony, poppy

Lucky Day of the Week: Tuesday

Most Compatible with: Leo, Sagittarius

Least Compatible with: Cancer, Libra, Capricorn

TAURUS

Taurus Key Traits: Loyal, dependable, patient, generous, stubborn, possessive, materialistic

Element: Earth

Animal: Bull

Body Parts Governed: Neck and throat

Ruling Planet: Venus

Lucky Numbers: 4, 6, 7, 8

Lucky Colors: Cream, green, orange, red, yellow

Lucky Gemstones: Coral, emerald, jade, sapphire, turquoise

Lucky Flower: Lily of the valley

Lucky Day of the Week: Friday

Most Compatible with: Virgo, Capricorn

Least Compatible with: Leo, Scorpio, Aquarius

GEMINI

Gemini Key Traits: Witty, energetic, imaginative, adaptable, fickle, restless, indecisive

Element: Air

Animal: Monkey

Body Parts Governed: Shoulders, arms, lungs

Ruling Planet: Mercury

Lucky Numbers: 3, 5, 8

Lucky Colors: Black, blue, white, yellow

Lucky Gemstones: Agate, aquamarine, tigereye, topaz

Lucky Flowers: Iris, lavender

Lucky Day of the Week: Wednesday

Most Compatible with: Libra, Aquarius

Least Compatible with: Virgo, Sagittarius, Pisces

CANCER

❖ Birthday: June 22–July 21 ❖

Cancer Key Traits: Perceptive, loyal, caring, dependable, moody, oversensitive, clingy

Element: Water

Animal: Crab

Body Parts Governed: Chest, breasts, stomach

Ruling Planet: Moon

Lucky Numbers: 2, 3, 5, 9

Lucky Colors: Black, indigo, pastel colors, silver

Lucky Gemstones: Amethyst, aquamarine, emerald

Lucky Flower: Water lily

Lucky Day of the Week: Monday

Most Compatible with: Scorpio, Pisces

Least Compatible with: Aries, Libra, Capricorn

LEO

Leo Key Traits: Ambitious, generous, confident, loyal, domineering, vain, overdramatic

Element: Fire

Animal: Lion

Body Parts Governed: Heart, upper back, spine

Ruling Planet: Sun

Lucky Numbers: 1, 3, 9

Lucky Colors: Black, gold, indigo, orange, red

Lucky Gemstones: Amber, diamond, sardonyx

Lucky Flower: Sunflower

Lucky Day of the Week: Sunday

Most Compatible with: Aries, Sagittarius

Least Compatible with: Taurus, Scorpio, Aquarius

VIRGO

❖ Birthday: August 22–September 21 ❖

Virgo Key Traits: Organized, reliable, helpful, analytical, rigid, particular, skeptical

Element: Earth

Animal: Magpie

Body Parts Governed: Liver, intestines, pancreas, gallbladder

Ruling Planet: Mercury

Lucky Numbers: 1, 3, 4, 6, 8

Lucky Colors: Blue, brown, green, orange, yellow

Lucky Gemstones: Agate, diamond, heliotrope, jasper

Lucky Flowers: Hyacinth, jasmine

Lucky Day of the Week: Wednesday

Most Compatible with: Taurus, Capricorn

Least Compatible with: Gemini, Sagittarius, Pisces

LIBRA

❖ Birthday: September 22–October 21 ❖

Libra Key Traits: Fair, idealistic, diplomatic, peaceful, indecisive, superficial, vain

Element: Air

Animal: Dove

Body Parts Governed: Adrenal glands, kidneys

Ruling Planet: Venus

Lucky Numbers: 1, 7, 8, 9

Lucky Colors: Blue, red, pale green, pink

Lucky Gemstones: Aquamarine, coral, emerald, jade, quartz, sapphire

Lucky Flowers: Rose, white lily

Lucky Day of the Week: Friday

Most Compatible with: Gemini, Aquarius

Least Compatible with: Aries, Cancer, Capricorn

SCORPIO

Scorpio Key Traits: Passionate, curious, loyal, resourceful, jealous, obsessive, inflexible

Element: Water

Animal: Scorpion

Body Parts Governed: Reproductive system, genitals

Ruling Planet: Pluto

Lucky Numbers: 2, 5, 7

Lucky Colors: Brown, green, red, purple

Lucky Gemstones: Amethyst, bloodstone, jasper, opal, topaz

Lucky Flowers: Cactus, chrysanthemum, white and blue gentian

Lucky Day of the Week: Tuesday

Most Compatible with: Cancer, Pisces

Least Compatible with: Taurus, Leo, Aquarius

SAGITTARIUS

❖ Birthday: November 22–December 21 ❖

Sagittarius Key Traits: Independent, caring, intellectual, fun-loving, innocent, moody, gullible

Element: Fire

Animal: Horse

Body Parts Governed: Hips, thighs

Ruling Planet: Jupiter

Lucky Numbers: 1, 3, 5, 9

Lucky Colors: Blue, red, orange, purple, yellow

Lucky Gemstones: Agate, amethyst, garnet, turquoise

Lucky Flower: Orchid

Lucky Day of the Week: Thursday

Most Compatible with: Aries, Leo

Least Compatible with: Gemini, Virgo, Pisces

CAPRICORN

❖ Birthday: December 22–January 21 ❖

Capricorn Key Traits: Ambitious, patient, responsible, loyal, domineering, self-absorbed, distrusting

Element: Earth

Animal: Goat

Body Parts Governed: Bones, joints, teeth, knees

Ruling Planet: Saturn

Lucky Numbers: 1, 2, 8

Lucky Colors: Black, brown, indigo, purple, silver

Lucky Gemstones: Agate, alexandrite, onyx, topaz, turquoise

Lucky Flower: Poppy

Lucky Day of the Week: Saturday

Most Compatible with: Taurus, Virgo

Least Compatible with: Aries, Cancer, Libra

AQUARIUS

Aquarius Key Traits: Forward-thinking, original, witty, humanitarian, aloof, rebellious, stubborn

Element: Air

Animal: Fox

Body Parts Governed: Circulatory system, calves, shins, ankles

Ruling Planet: Uranus

Lucky Numbers: 1, 2, 4

Lucky Colors: Blue, gray, orange, pink

Lucky Gemstones: Garnet, opal, sapphire, turquoise

Lucky Flowers: Foxglove, snowdrop

Lucky Day of the Week: Saturday

Most Compatible with: Gemini, Libra

Least Compatible with: Taurus, Leo, Scorpio

PISCES

❖ Birthday: February 22–March 21 ❖

Pisces Key Traits: Compassionate, devoted, accepting, imaginative, oversensitive, lazy, escapist

Element: Water

Animal: Fish

Body Parts Governed: Immune system, feet

Ruling Planet: Neptune

Lucky Numbers: 2, 4, 5, 6

Lucky Colors: Blue, gray, green

Lucky Gemstones: Amethyst, carnelian, diamond

Lucky Flowers: Iris, water lily

Lucky Day of the Week: Thursday

Most Compatible with: Cancer, Scorpio

Least Compatible with: Gemini, Virgo, Sagittarius

CHINESE ZODIAC

Using the Chinese Zodiac (an astrological system based on birth year) is another way to divine the personality and future of your baby. Which zodiac animals will your baby get along with best?

IF YOU WERE BORN IN . . .	YOUR CHINESE ZODIAC ANIMAL IS . . .
1912, 1924, 1936, 1948, 1960, 1972, 1984, 1996, 2008	Rat
1913, 1925, 1937, 1949, 1961, 1973, 1985, 1997, 2009	Ox
1914, 1926, 1938, 1950, 1962, 1974, 1986, 1998, 2010	Tiger
1915, 1927, 1939, 1951, 1963, 1975, 1987, 1999, 2011	Rabbit
1916, 1928, 1940, 1952, 1964, 1976, 1988, 2000, 2012	Dragon
1917, 1929, 1941, 1953, 1965, 1977, 1989, 2001, 2013	Snake
1918, 1930, 1942, 1954, 1966, 1978, 1990, 2002, 2014	Horse
1919, 1931, 1943, 1955, 1967, 1979, 1991, 2003, 2015	Sheep (Ram or Goat)
1920, 1932, 1944, 1956, 1968, 1980, 1992, 2004, 2016	Monkey
1921, 1933, 1945, 1957, 1969, 1981, 1993, 2005, 2017	Rooster
1922, 1934, 1946, 1958, 1970, 1982, 1994, 2006, 2018	Dog
1923, 1935, 1947, 1959, 1971, 1983, 1995, 2007, 2019	Pig

RAT

Key Rat Traits: Charming, funny, generous, kind, selfish, impatient

Most Compatible with: Dragon, Monkey

Least Compatible with: Horse

OX

Key Ox Traits: Protective, patient, kind, methodical, egotistical, stifling

Most Compatible with: Snake, Rooster

Least Compatible with: Sheep

TIGER

Key Tiger Traits: Warmhearted, passionate, devoted, fearless, restless, moody

Most Compatible with: Horse, Dog

Least Compatible with: Monkey

RABBIT

Key Rabbit Traits: Gentle, nurturing, flexible, family oriented, soft spoken, conflict averse

Most Compatible with: Sheep, Pig

Least Compatible with: Rooster

DRAGON

Key Dragon Traits: Decisive, passionate, authoritative, charismatic, distractible, self-centered

Most Compatible with: Snake, Rooster

Least Compatible with: Sheep

SNAKE

Key Snake Traits: Wise, imaginative, attractive, creative, vain, uncommunicative

Most Compatible with: Rooster, Ox

Least Compatible with: Pig

HORSE

Key Horse Traits: Magnetic, intelligent, open-minded, diligent, stubborn, condescending

Most Compatible with: Tiger, Dog

Least Compatible with: Rat

SHEEP

Key Sheep Traits: Nurturing, creative, loyal, stable, oversenstive, insecure

Most Compatible with: Rabbit, Pig

Least Compatible with: Ox

MONKEY

Key Monkey Traits: Empathetic, fun loving, inquisitive, energetic, manipulative, fickle

Most Compatible with: Dragon, Rat

Least Compatible with: Tiger

ROOSTER

Key Rooster Traits: Straightforward, organized, confident, detail oriented, boastful, moody

Most Compatible with: Snake, Ox

Least Compatible with: Rabbit

DOG

Key Dog Traits: Faithful, empathetic, inspiring, shy, worrisome, judgmental

Most Compatible with: Tiger, Horse

Least Compatible with: Dragon

PIG

Key Pig Traits: Curious, honest, tolerant, well-mannered, materialistic, naive

Most Compatible with: Sheep, Rabbit

Least Compatible with: Snake

SECTION 3: BABY'S HERE!

"A babe in the house is a well-spring of pleasure, a messenger of peace and love, a resting place for innocence on earth, a link between angels and men."
—Martin Farquhar Tupper

Everything changes after baby is born. In this chapter, you will learn what to do to keep baby safe and to help establish a positive future for him or her. From choosing a name to watching baby grow, your actions have consequences—make sure they are the best ones.

BRINGING BABY HOME

Here are a few things you can do to maximize baby's good fortune and foretell his or her destiny.

When bringing baby home from the hospital, it is bad luck to sit in the backseat with her unless there are no other seats available. Bring another person with you in the car so you can ride in back, or ride in the front seat.

When baby comes home, carry him upstairs before you go downstairs. This will ensure that his luck in life always rises instead of going down. If you are leaving a hospital with baby, make sure you walk up stairs or go up in the elevator before going down, for the same reasons. If no stairs are at hand, makeshift stairs may be improvised by stepping up on a sturdy box.

When you arrive home with baby, carry her around the house three times. This will help ease any future bouts of colic. Next, carry her to the attic or highest point in the house—this will ensure she becomes an upstanding citizen.

The first meal at home after baby is born should be a large, celebratory one, in which everyone eats, drinks, and toasts to baby's future good fortune.

The first object that a child reaches for is very important, as it may determine his destiny. Reaching for a piece of food, for example, could mean that baby will have a career as a chef; a newborn who stretches out his hand for a ball may be a professional athlete; and an infant who touches clothing may have fashion design in her future.

Baby's relationship with money can be determined by putting a coin on a table or on the floor near where he is. If he reaches for the coin, he will have money all his life. If he ignores the coin, he will be frugal with his money.

If you put a coin into a newborn's hand and her fist closes over it, she will always love money and be prosperous. If her fist does not close, or if she drops the coin, she will be often short on cash.

Place baby on the floor with a Bible, a dollar, and a deck of cards. If he chooses the Bible, he will be religious; reaching for the dollar means he will be financially successful; and if the deck of cards is chosen, he will take risks in life that will usually pay off.

BABY GIFTS

Friends and family will be excited to meet baby and will arrive bearing gifts for mother and child. Here are gift ideas that hold special meaning.

For luck, give a newborn a gift of bread or salt. Add an egg to the gift to signify that baby will always have the essentials in life.

Matches keep away bad spirits and supernatural occurrences—presented along with a candle, they make a lovely gift.

Hard-boiled eggs, especially dyed red, are good luck and bring long life and future fertility.

Coral protects against the evil eye—a necklace for the new mother with coral in it will keep the infant safe.

Silver brings good fortune—give baby a piece of silver to ensure his or her luck.

Plant a tree when baby is born—as the tree grows, so will the child. Traditionally, an apple tree is planted for a boy and a pear tree for a girl. For twins, plant two trees.

BABY'S LOOKS

To you, your baby will be perfect. But a baby's specific features can provide insight into his or her future, so take a closer look.

ATTRACTIVENESS

A pretty infant will be less attractive when he grows up, while a homely baby will acquire great beauty.

BELLY BUTTON

A newborn with an "outie" belly button will have to work hard for money.

A baby with an "innie" belly button will have success and happiness.

BIRTHMARKS AND OTHER DISTINGUISHING FEATURES

Birthmarks on the right side of the body portend better luck than those on the left side.

A birthmark shaped like a bird or a cross means your child will be lucky and blessed.

A wheel-shaped birthmark will bring luck to its owner.

A birthmark on baby's leg means he will travel far and wide.

A birthmark on baby's arm means she will be strong.

A birthmark on baby's face portends future beauty.

A birthmark in the shape of an object on baby means that the mother-to-be stole that object when she was pregnant.

This old rhyme explains the meaning behind moles or other marks on a newborn's body:

A mole on the neck,
You'll have money by the peck.
A mole on the ear,
You'll have money by the year.
A mole on the lip,
You're a little too flip.
A mole on your arm,
You'll never be harmed.
A mole on your back,
You'll have money by the sack.

CHEST

A baby born with a rash on her chest will be healthy all her life.

CHIN

An infant whose chin sticks out will have a bad temper.

EARS

Babies with large ears are thought to grow up to become generous adults and very eloquent speakers.

Wide and thick ears foretell prosperity.

Long ears mean your child will be wise.

Babies with very small ears will never be rich.

HAIR

Babies born with a lot of hair will have some difficulty in life.

Babies born bald will grow up to have sharp wit and intelligence.

Children born with curly hair have fairy powers.

Newborns with a double cowlick will be headstrong, stubborn, and mischievous, but always lucky. One cowlick denotes a less strong personality—but also less luck.

If your baby's hairline forms a ducktail, your next baby will be a girl. If the hairline is straight across, a boy will be your next child.

HANDS

When a baby is born with open hands and outstretched fingers, it is said to be a sign that he or she will enjoy a great deal of prosperity but will also be generous with wealth.

A child born with tightly closed fists will be stingy later in life.

Hands that are big for baby's body mean he will be skilled in manual labor.

Long fingers indicate artistic and musical talent.

MOUTH

A large mouth on an infant means she has the makings of a good singer.

RESEMBLANCES

A baby boy who resembles his mother will have life-long luck.

SKIN

Infants with reddish skin will have fiery tempers.

TEETH

It is believed that if a newborn comes into the world with teeth, she could be a vampire. Luckily, teeth at birth are very uncommon!

A baby who grows teeth before six months of age may be a selfish child.

WHAT'S IN A NAME?

A baby's name is one of the first things given to him or her. But choose wisely, for names can spell destiny.

FOR BEAUTY

GIRL NAMES
Alana
Annabelle
Astrid
Belinda
Bella
Caitlin
Caroline
Kyla
Leila
Liliana

BOY NAMES
Adonis
Alan
Cullen
Finn
Irving
Jamal
Kenneth

FOR HAPPINESS

GIRL NAMES
Abigail
Alicia
Blythe
Elizabeth
Felicia
Hilary
Lara
Tatum
Thalia

BOY NAMES
Asher
Felix
Gil
Lear
Merrill
Ronen
Shankar

FOR KINDNESS AND GENEROSITY

GIRL NAMES
Aloha
Eleanor
Leonora
Leora
Mercy
Mildred
Rebecca

BOY NAMES
Aidan
Anand
Clement
Jonathan
Kannon
Kieran
Kyrie
Racham

FOR LOVE

GIRL NAMES
Amanda
Amy
Carissa
Clare
Elaine
Esme
Leilani
Marian
Seraphina
Valentina

BOY NAMES
Ames
Byron
Craddock
Darrell
David
Jed
Phillip
Tristan
Zane

FOR LOYALTY

GIRL NAMES
Constance
Faith
Fidelity
Germaine
Ivy
Lela
Marianne

BOY NAMES
Absalom
Andreas
Abdul
Bond
Caleb
Campbell
Jerome

FOR POWER AND STRENGTH

GIRL NAMES

Audrey
Brianna
Brigitte
Carla
Delilah
Devi
Kendra
Stephanie

BOY NAMES

Aaron
Aubrey
Blaise
Cyrus
Easton
Emery
Ethan
Joseph
Theodore
Wyatt

FOR SUCCESS

GIRL NAMES
Aliya
Barika
Elisha
Emily
Helga
Radha

BOY NAMES
Cedric
Dean
Eli
Emmett
Frederick
Jonas
Neil
Rodrigo
Sterling

FOR WEALTH

GIRL NAMES
Ada
Adriana
Daria
Edith
Elodie
Jessalyn
Jessica
Odette

BOY NAMES
Darius
Eaton
Edward
Francis
Jesse
McKeon
Otto
Richard

FOR WISDOM

GIRL NAMES
Athena
Aubrey
Dara
Jada
Kaya
Sage
Sonia
Sophie

BOY NAMES
Aldo
Alfred
Connor
Conrad
Elvis
Nestor
Sebastian
Solomon
Ray

NAMES FOR LUCK

It is lucky to give a baby the same or a similar name as the person who attends or assists the birth. So learn the names of those doctors, nurses, and midwives!

If a child is born on a saint's day, it is good luck to give him or her the name (or a derivation) of that saint.

It is lucky for a child's initials to spell out a word.

The luckiest boys' names have an even number of syllables, while it is more fortunate for girls to have names with an odd number of syllables.

A boy with a four-syllable name will always be loyal and dependable.

It is bad luck for a child to have 13 letters in his or her name; avoid this at all costs.

And, above all, choose the name carefully, for it is bad luck to change a baby's name once it has been decided upon.

NAME NUMEROLOGY

Just as numerology was used in the previous section to determine baby's traits based on birth date, so too can numerology work when it comes to a child's name.

You can determine baby's number based on his or her full name (or if you are still deciding on names, try out several to see what numbers they add up to). Refer to the chart below—you will see that each number, 1 through 9, has corresponding letters beneath it.

1	2	3	4	5	6	7	8	9
A	B	C	D	E	F	G	H	I
J	K	L	M	N	O	P	Q	R
S	T	U	V	W	X	Y	Z	

Write out baby's full (including middle) name.

For example,

MARY CLARA SMITH

Now, following the chart, place a corresponding number under each letter.

M A R Y   C L A R A   S M I T H
4 1 9 7   3 3 1 9 1   1 4 9 2 8

Now add together the numbers for each of the names. If the result is a two-digit number, add those numbers together.

$4 + 1 + 9 + 7 = 21 \rightarrow 2 + 1 = 3$

$3 + 3 + 1 + 9 + 1 = 17 \rightarrow 1 + 7 = 8$

$1 + 4 + 9 + 2 + 8 = 24 \rightarrow 2 + 4 = 6$

Finally, add those three numbers together. Again, if the result is two digits, add those digits so the result is a one-digit number—unless the result is 11 or 22. Those numbers are "master numbers" that have special significance.

$3 + 8 + 6 = 17 \rightarrow 1 + 7 = 8$

8 is the result.

Here is what the numbers mean:

1 = Creative, independent, original, adventurous,
     yet egotistical

2 = Empathetic, diplomatic, sensitive, intuitive, cautious,
     yet codependent

3 = Artistic, enthusiastic, visionary, optimistic, sociable,
     yet superficial and wasteful

4 = Organized, efficient, practical, loyal, serious, yet rigid

5 = Creative, inventive, free-spirited, adaptable,
     yet volatile

6 = Responsible, understanding, loving, passionate,
     harmonious, yet jealous

7 = Intuitive, spiritual, wise, analytical, yet critical
     and isolated

8 = Powerful, decisive, authoritative, organized,
     yet materialistic

9 = Compassionate, generous, romantic, imaginative,
     devoted, yet overemotional

11 and 22 are "master numbers" and their characteristics are as follows:

11 = Creative, idealistic, inventive, wise, yet insensitive. An 11 can also have characteristics of a 2, since 1 + 1 = 2.

22 = Innovative, driven, practical, masterful, yet harsh. A 22 can also have characteristics of a 4, since 2 + 2 = 4.

CARING FOR BABY

While feeding, bathing, and dressing baby are necessary daily routines, you can make the most of them by heeding the advice on the following pages.

BATHING

To augur good fortune for baby, place the following in her first bathwater:

❖ A coin for future wealth

❖ An egg for strength

❖ Sugar for a sweet and well-rounded character

❖ Salt for eloquence

❖ Bread for good luck

Give baby a cold bath on Easter Sunday, and he will have good health for the rest of the year.

During baby's first bath, put a little water in her mouth, and she will grow to be a good swimmer.

Washing a child's right hand before he is three days old will take away his future riches. Save the first bath for baby's fourth day of life.

An infant's bathtub must never be used for any other purpose, or it will bring bad financial luck to the family.

Use the water from baby's first bath to water a tree—both the tree and the baby will grow strong. Or throw the bathwater over a flowering plant, and baby will be an attractive child and adult.

DRESSING

For good luck, dress a baby for the first time from his feet up, not over his head.

The first clothing put on a child should be new, not a hand-me-down.

Dress your newborn in clothes for the opposite sex from time to time (put a baby boy in pink clothes and a girl in blue clothes) to confuse evil spirits who might want to steal the baby's soul. Alternatively, dress baby in neutral-colored clothing.

Clothes put on inside out are lucky. . . . If you do it accidentally, do not change them.

It is bad luck to dress an infant in black.

Mending or patching baby's clothing while she is still wearing it invites bad luck.

It is better luck to put on both of baby's socks first and then both his shoes, rather than sock/shoe, sock/shoe.

Always put clothes on the right side first (socks and shoes on the right foot, pants on the right leg, shirts on the right arm).

If a newborn wears clothes passed down from an older baby, she will not cry at night.

FEEDING

If baby is offered the right breast first, he will be right-handed, and vice versa. After the very first feeding, always begin with the left breast, as it will make baby wise and loyal.

Breast milk smoothed over a newborn's brow will make her eyebrows thick and lush.

A baby who cries constantly is often thought to be expressing a need for something his mother craved during pregnancy but was denied. Give that thing to him and the crying will cease.

Feeding red apple to an infant will give her rosy cheeks (remove the skin first).

When baby begins to feed himself, encourage him to do so with his right hand; the left hand is unlucky.

If a newborn spills milk, she should never be scolded; it is bad luck. (This is the derivation of the adage "don't cry over spilled milk"!)

It is bad luck to wean a baby in early spring; wait until all the snows have melted and flowers have bloomed.

CARING FOR YOURSELF

While taking care of your new baby will be your utmost concern, be sure to take time to look after yourself. Read on for particular precautions and actions you can take.

The first bite a new mother eats after giving birth should come from her partner's spoon; it will speed her healing.

New mothers should not be left alone in their homes during the first six weeks following childbirth, for the devil then has more power over them. Have friends or family with you in the house at all times.

A woman recovering from childbirth may not look out of her bedroom window for six weeks, or else every vehicle that she sees pass by may take a bit of luck with it.

Anyone who carries a basket into the room of a woman recovering from childbirth must break a splinter from it and place it in the baby's cradle, otherwise the basket holder will carry away the mother's or child's peace and quiet.

A woman may not enter a stranger's house for six weeks following the birth of her child. If she does so, she should first buy something in another village, or she will bring misfortune into the house.

PROTECTING BABY

Make sure baby is safe from harm by minding the counsel on the following pages.

Rub baby's feet with mother's milk to protect him and to make him strong.

Make sure baby's feet are covered while she is sleeping, lest her soul escape.

Placing sweets under a new mother's bed will occupy any lurking evil spirits and keep them away from baby.

A mirror in a child's room will keep away fairies and bad spirits, which avoid mirrors because they cannot stand to see their own reflection.

Tie a red ribbon or cord around baby's wrist; this will protect him from spells and curses. Red clothing has the same effect.

A mixture of salt and pepper, sprinkled around the house where a newborn dwells, will offer protection to all inhabitants, especially the newborn.

Bells offer protection from witches and demons; hang wind chimes outside baby's window, or a bell over her crib.

During the first six weeks following childbirth, new mothers should avoid going to sleep alone in the same room as baby. If you must, lay a pair of men's pants over the cradle for protection, or wrap baby in one of her father's garments.

To keep an infant from being bewitched, pass him three times over a stack of his mother's clothing.

A broom near baby's crib will keep demons and evil spirits away.

Rosemary is a protective herb; plant some in a garden or window box to keep a child safe.

Fennel protects baby from illness; place some fennel seed or fennel oil in her bath.

Lilacs drive away evil spirits; plant some in your garden, or put cut blooms in a vase.

Have a man jump over baby on the floor. This will ensure that baby has a safe childhood.

Place a knife, a ball of yarn, and a key under an infant's cradle to ward off evil spirits. Alternately, place a bag of salt in the cradle.

Carry a black marble for baby's protection from the evil eye at night, and a white marble during the day.

Money, beer, and tobacco placed around a house keep evil spirits from harming a newborn.

Amber beads protect baby from illness.

Blue beads keep witches away.

Shell necklaces protect children and babies.

Small lizards are a good omen; their presence protects baby from harm. You might consider getting a new pet!

GENERAL BABY SUPERSTITIONS

Do not take a baby younger than forty days old to a cemetery; she will be vulnerable to spirits.

Just after baby is born, touch his mouth to the mother's left foot. This will ensure that he is loyal and not rebellious.

An infant who is licked by a dog will be a quick healer all her life.

Hearing seagulls or cranes during the first week of baby's life is a sign that he may be fussy and cry a lot.

For the child to cry at the christening is considered a fortunate sign—it means that evil spirits are leaving the baby's body.

If a newborn has a cold, sit with her on a beach where the tide is coming in—when the tide goes out, it will take away her illness with it.

Do not look upon baby from behind or he will become cross-eyed.

If it rains on baby while a rainbow is in the sky, she will get freckles.

It is bad luck to let baby look into a mirror before he is one year old.

Do not cut baby's nails until she is one month old.

If a teakettle boils in a room where a baby is, the baby will have colic.

Neither fire, salt, nor bread may be taken away from the house of a woman during the first six weeks following childbirth—this could bring harm to baby.

Mothers should not handle dough before their babies are six weeks old; it will make the baby's hands chap.

Kissing a baby on the hands or while he is asleep will make him oversensitive.

Kissing an infant on the back of the neck too much will make a disobedient child.

It is unlucky to place a newborn on a table without having one hand on him at all times.

If a visitor makes fun of your baby in any way, even in a joking manner, he will soon find the thing he mocks has become a part of him.

Never step over a baby who is crawling; it will stunt her growth.

Rubbing a small amount of honey on a newborn's head will bring her luck.

Rubbing apple on baby's tongue will make him a good singer.

When taking baby out of the house to visit friends or relatives, call ahead to make sure that those you are visiting are in good moods. The disposition of a boy baby will be affected by the man of the house, and a girl baby by the woman of the house.

It is bad luck to count a baby's teeth.

It is a good omen if an infant sneezes in your presence.

It is good luck to see a baby smile in her sleep.

To bring luck to a baby, rub his head with money, brush his body with a rabbit's foot, or put a string of beads around his neck.

Horseshoes hung in a newborn's room bring good luck, and also good dreams.

BABY'S GROWING!

Baby's milestones are thrilling occasions. Help ensure that these milestones go smoothly by heeding the following guidelines.

TALKING

Tickling the feet of a baby will cause her to grow up with a speech problem or a stutter.

Bathe newborns in rainwater and they will become good conversationalists.

Babies who play with rattles too much will be slow to talk. To encourage your child to talk, hold him up to a mirror (after his first birthday, of course!).

Rubbing a chicken's tongue on baby's lips will make her an eloquent speaker.

Kissing an infant on the lips will make her speak sooner.

TEETHING

Tap a baby's first tooth with a silver spoon to bring future wealth to him.

The longer a baby has to wait for her teeth to come in, the longer they will stay in mouth in old age.

Hang a coral necklace in baby's room to ensure easy teething.

To ease pain from teething, rub a newborn's gums with your wedding ring.

If a woman sticks pins or needles into curtains during the first six weeks after childbirth, her child will have bad teeth.

WALKING

Kissing an infant on the feet will make him walk early.

If baby is slow to walk, rub the backs of her legs with egg whites.

Embroider a cat motif on a child's clothing or shoes when he is just beginning to walk, and he will be as sure-footed as a cat.

BABY RITUALS AROUND THE WORLD

After childbirth, Burmese women eat a soup of plants, fish, and fruit.

Mexican mothers take steam baths after birth to relieve soreness, while Southeast Asian mothers light fires in their homes to serve the same purpose.

The Arapesh people of Papua New Guinea give fresh coconut meat to breast-feeding mothers; other than that, coconut is reserved for tribal feasts.

Tsinghai women in China carry their babies with them for up to five years—and breast-feed for the same amount of time.

Mayan mothers sleep holding their newborns and are never apart from them until the babies are twenty days old.

In the Philippines, it is customary for new mothers to eat the placenta soon after childbirth, served with boiled chicken and corn porridge.

Mexican parents in the Yucatán Peninsula typically pierce their girl babies' ears within an hour of the birth, believing that babies do not feel pain until their second day of life.

In the Yoruban culture of West Africa, twins are believed to bring health, prosperity, and happiness to the entire community. The birth of twins is an occasion for celebration, and large feasts are organized. The firstborn twin is called Taiwo, which means "having the first taste of the world," and the second-born is called Kehinde, meaning "arriving after the other." The Yorubans believe that firstborn twins are more adventurous, brave, and curious, while second-born twins are more careful, intelligent, and self-reflective.

Throughout Africa, bowls of food are set in front of eight-day-old twins, and a spell is chanted to help the twins keep their families safe from harm.

A SLEEPING BABY

Everyone has heard the adage "never wake a sleeping baby"; here are some more pieces of advice and portents on baby's slumber.

Never sweep or dust in baby's room while she is asleep; when baby sleeps, her soul leaves the body briefly, and you do not want to sweep it away.

Clear all tables before putting baby down to sleep, otherwise his sleep will be restless.

When an infant smiles in its sleep, angels are talking to it.

If a newborn is first laid on its left side, it will grow up to become a clumsy child and adult.

Babies sleep best when their feet are pointing south and their heads are pointing north.

Never rock an empty cradle; it steals baby's sleep away.

Baby's bed may be changed on any day but Friday. Friday changing will bring bad dreams.

HOW BABY SLEEPS

If baby sleeps in a fetal position, she will grow up to be sensitive and shy but with a tough exterior.

If baby sleeps on his back with his arms close to his body, he will be a reserved and quiet adult who has high standards for himself and others.

If baby sleeps on her side with arms and feet pointing straight down, she will be a social, outgoing, and trusting person as she grows.

If baby sleeps on his side with his arms extended, he will be open-minded, though a little suspicious and stubborn.

If baby sleeps on her belly, with her arms underneath her body and her head turned to the side, she will be brave, gregarious, and likable.

If baby sleeps on his back with his arms above his head, he will be a good listener and a helpful friend, though he will be uncomfortable in the spotlight.

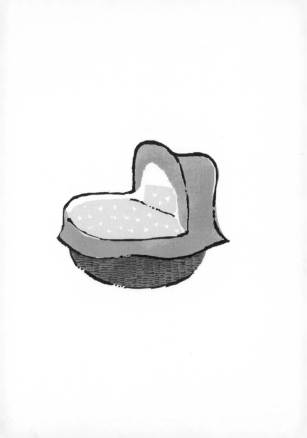

BABY BLESSINGS

Recite one or more of these blessings to welcome your new arrival into your home and your life.

JEWISH BABY BLESSING

In every birth, blessed is the wonder.
In every creation, blessed is the new beginning.
In every child, blessed is life.
In every hope, blessed is the potential.
In every transition, blessed is the beginning.
In every existence, blessed are the possibilities.
In every love, blessed are the tears.
In every life, blessed is the love.

BUDDHIST BABY BLESSING

May all calamities be warded off,
may all illness be dispelled,
may no obstacles hinder me,
may you live long and happily.
May all good fortune come your way,
may all the deities protect you,
by all the power of the Buddha
may you always enjoy well-being.
May all good fortune come your way,
may all the deities protect you,
by all the power of the Dhamma
may you always enjoy well-being.
May all good fortune come your way,
may all the deities protect you,
by all the power of the Sangha
may you always enjoy well-being.

By the power of these protective verses,
may your misfortunes be destroyed,
troubles due to stars and demons,
harmful spirits and ominous planets.
May rain fall in due time,
may there be a rich harvest,
may the world be prosperous,
may the government be righteous.
By the power of all mighty Buddhas,
you secure protection in every way.

IRISH BABY BLESSING #1

May you be blessed with
the strength of heaven,
the light of the sun
and the radiance of the moon,
the splendor of fire,
the speed of lightning,
the swiftness of wind,
the depth of the sea,
the stability of earth,
and the firmness of rock.

IRISH BABY BLESSING #2

May all the blessing of our Lord
touch your life today.
May He send His little angels
to protect you on your way.
Such a wee little fit, sent from above,
Someone so precious to cherish and love.
May sunshine and moonbeams
dance over your head,
As you quietly slumber in your bed.
May good luck be with you wherever you go,
And your blessings outnumber
the shamrocks that grow.

IRISH BABY BLESSING #3

May you always walk in sunshine.
May you never want for more.
May Irish angels rest their wings
beside your nursery door.
And for the proud parents:
May God grant you
a wee bit of heaven
to cradle in your arms—
a sweet bonny baby
to hold close to your heart.
A newborn babe
brings light to the house,
warmth to the hearth,
and joy to the soul.
For wealth is family,
family is wealth.

NONDENOMINATIONAL BABY BLESSING

Dearest baby, born of two hearts,
You are grace,
You are beauty,
You are love beyond measure,
And gift without price.
We are gathered this day
To introduce you to your greater family,
And to bless you, before the world,
Even as we have been blessed by your birth!
We offer you to the Four Winds
That you might embrace adventure
And know the wonder of far-off lands.
We offer you to the Sky
That you may steer by the stars
And never feel that you are far from home.
We offer you to the Sun
That warmth and light may surround you always
And guide you safely on your way.
We offer you to the Moon
That you may find comfort in darkness
And never have cause to fear the night.

NATIVE AMERICAN BABY BLESSING

Sun, Moon, Stars, all you that move in the heavens,
hear us!
Into your midst has come a new life.
Make his/her path smooth,
that he/she may reach the brow of the first hill!
Winds, Clouds, Rain, Mist,
all you that move in the air, hear us!
Into your midst has come a new life.
Make his/her path smooth,
that he/she may reach the brow of the second hill!
Hills, Valleys, Rivers, Lakes, Trees, Grasses,
all you of the earth, hear us!
Into your midst has come a new life.
Make his/her path smooth,
that he/she may reach the brow of the third hill!

Birds, great and small, that fly in the air,
Animals, great and small, that dwell in the forest,
Insects that creep among the grasses and burrow in
the ground, hear us!
Into your midst has come a new life.
Make his/her path smooth,
that he/she may reach the brow of the fourth hill!
All you of the heavens, all you of the air,
all you of the earth, hear us!
Into your midst has come a new life.
Make his/her path smooth,
then shall he/she travel beyond the four hills!

HINDU BABY BLESSING

If baby only wanted to,
he could fly up to heaven this moment.
It is not for nothing that he does not leave us.
He loves to rest his head on mother's bosom,
and cannot ever bear to lose sight of her.
Baby knows all manner of wise words,
though few on earth can understand their meaning.
It is not for nothing that he never wants to speak.
The one thing he wants is to
learn mother's words from mother's lips.
That is why he looks so innocent.
Baby had a heap of gold and pearls,
yet he came like a beggar on to this earth.
It is not for nothing he came in such a disguise.
This dear little naked mendicant
pretends to be utterly helpless,
so that he may beg for mother's wealth of love.
Baby was so free from every tie
in the land of the tiny crescent moon.
It was not for nothing he gave up his freedom.

He knows that there is room for endless joy
in mother's little corner of a heart,
and it is sweeter far than liberty to be
caught and pressed in her dear arms.
Baby never knew how to cry.
He dwelt in the land of perfect bliss.
It is not for nothing he has chosen to shed tears.
Though with the smile of his dear face
he draws mother's yearning heart to him,
yet his little cries over tiny troubles
weave the double bond of pity and love.

ABOUT BABY

Baby's Name _____

Birthday _____

Time of Birth _____

Weight _____

Length _____

Library of Congress Cataloging-in-Publishing Data available.

ISBN 978-0-8118-7935-4

Manufactured in China
Design by Cat Grishaver
Text by K. C. Jones

The advice and instruction in this book is meant for entertainment
purposes only. Always consult with your doctor or other medical
professional before making any change to your pregnancy and child-
care routines. The author and Chronicle Books hereby disclaim any
and all liability resulting from injuries or damage caused by following
any recommendations contained in this book.

Also available in this series: Fortune-Telling Book of Names, Fortune-
Telling Book of Dreams, Fortune-Telling Book for Brides, Fortune-
Telling Book of the Zodiac, and Fortune-Telling Birthday Book.

10 9 8 7 6 5 4 3 2 1

Chronicle Books LLC
680 Second Street
San Francisco, CA 94107
www.chroniclebooks.com

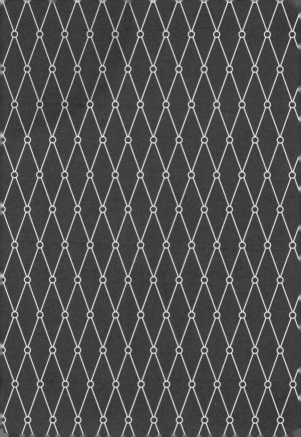

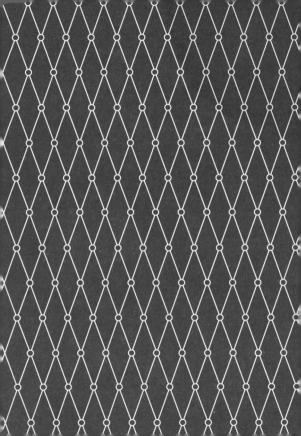